SEVEN YOUTH GROUP SESSIONS ON
1 THESSALONIANS

NICK MARGESSON

CF4·K

10 9 8 7 6 5 4 3 2 1

ISBN: 978-1-84550-462-5
© 2009 Nick Margesson
Edited by David Jackman and Thalia Blundell

Published in 2009 by
Christian Focus Publications, Geanies House, Fearn,
Tain, Ross-shire, IV20 1TW, Great Britain.
www.christianfocus.com
Cover design by Daniel van Straaten
Printed by Bell and Bain, Glasgow

Scripture quotations used in this book are from the Holy Bible, New
International Version. Copyright © 1973, 1978, 1984, International
Bible Society. Used by permission of Zondervan Bible Publishers.

Mixed Sources
Product group from well-managed
forests and other controlled sources
www.fsc.org Cert no. TT-COC-002769
© 1996 Forest Stewardship Council
FSC

CONTENTS

INTRODUCTION

As a youth leader you have the great privilege of introducing young people to the Lord Jesus Christ and helping them to grow in the Christian faith. The 14-18s age group are at the junction between the younger teens and the adult church and this is often where we lose them. The Junction is a series of books designed to help you teach older teens to study the Bible in a way which is challenging and intellectually stretching. Because they are often unprepared to take things at face value and are encouraged to question everything, it is important to satisfy the mind while touching the heart. The ready-to-use sessions contained in the books are for youth groups of varying sizes, with normal leaders and normal teenagers who want to serve an awesome God.

Each book in the series contains one teaching module, which will normally last from 4-7 weeks. At the front of the book is an overview of the Bible teaching, which can be photocopied for your church leader so that he/she is aware of what is being taught. Each lesson plan, in addition to a lesson aim, contains study notes to enable the leader to understand the Bible passage, a slot to encourage the young people to share experiences and learn from each other, a suggestion to focus attention on the study to follow, suggestions for a prayer and praise time and an optional work-sheet to help the young people engage with the passage. Recognising that youth groups vary in size and available space every effort has been made to include activities that are easily adaptable.

Putting Together a Youth Group Session

What should we include in our youth group sessions?

If you wander into any Christian bookshop and ask the question, "What should we include in our youth group sessions?" you had better be prepared for a very long stay in the bookshop! Just about every book on youth ministry that you pick up off the shelf will give you a different answer to that question – generally based on the author's preference, upbringing, experiences, etc. Interestingly, if you pick up your Bible and ask the same question you will also be in for a long wait, because, as far as I can see, the Bible never mentions youth groups, let alone what might be involved in a youth group session. In fact, the Bible very rarely makes any distinction between particular groupings of Christians – it talks about all Christians and makes no particular distinction about age or nationality or background, etc.

So, if our youth group is a Christian youth group, then the question we really need to ask is, "What does it look like when Christians (of any age) get together?" And, on this subject, the Bible has plenty to say! One of the most complete descriptions of what this looks like in practice comes in Acts 2:42-47, where we are given a fairly detailed description of what the earliest group of believers was like. Whenever God's people got together, they engaged in a whole variety of activities – they prayed together, they praised God together, they learned from God's word together, they reminded each other of what God had done for them, they cared practically for each other, they spent plenty of time together, they cared for the world around them, they proclaimed the good news of Jesus, and so on. You could sum it up by saying that they were devoted to God and devoted to each other. And, interestingly, this type of devotion was clearly very attractive to the world around them – "the Lord added to their number daily those who were being saved" (Acts 2:47).

If our youth group is a Christian youth group then, in a youth appropriate way, we need to be displaying that same devotion to God and to each other whenever we meet together. What elements in our youth group sessions will help our groups to do this?

- **Time** – it is noticeable in Acts 2 how much time the early believers spent together. They met together daily in the temple courts, they ate together, they hung out at each others' homes.

  With busy teenagers and busy leaders, spending this much time together would be impossible for just about every youth group, but relationships are a key element of being devoted to one another, and relationships need time and space to develop. In our programming we need to allow time and space for young people and leaders to hang out together.

  Food is a great way to get people to spend time together and, again, it does not have to be complicated or fancy – a bag of doughnuts or some cheese toasties or a pizza are not difficult to arrange.

  In the session outlines in this material, we have not included hang-out time because the way it works best will be different for each group. The hang-out time does not have to be particularly structured but it does need to happen.

- **Teaching** – in Acts 2 we are told that the believers devoted themselves to the Apostles' teaching (verse 42). The Apostles were commissioned by Jesus to be the authoritative teachers of the early church (John 15:26-27). In the New Testament, the Apostles' teaching is authenticated as God's word through signs and wonders (Acts 2:43).

  Of course, today, we have the amazing privilege of being able to listen to the Apostles' teaching and so listen to God's word whenever the Bible is opened and read and studied. Being devoted to God must, at least, mean listening to his word and trying to put it into practice in our lives. This is why really good Bible teaching needs to be at the centre of our youth group sessions.

  In the session outlines in this material, the 'Bible Time' is one of the key elements to the session. There will usually be a couple of components to the 'Bible Time' – an introductory Bible activity (Focus) followed by a short Bible study.

  For more help on teaching the Bible to young people, please see '7 top tips for teaching the Bible to young people' on page 10.

- **Sharing & Testimony** – one of the ways that Christians show that they are devoted to one another is by getting to know one another and by listening and learning from each other. In our youth group sessions it is great to be able to programme in times where people can get to know each other a bit better. That might be by running a simple mixer activity or by interviewing somebody or by asking people to share their experiences or thoughts on a particular topic or issue.

  In the session outlines in this material we have included a 'Talk Time' in each session. Sometimes these 'Talk Times' are specifically linked to the teaching topic for that session and sometimes they just refer to general issues facing Christians.

We have also included an optional 'Getting to Know You' slot in each session. If your group members already know each other really well then you may decide that this activity is unnecessary.

- **Prayer** – One of the most foundational activities that Christians engage in when they meet together is prayer. Prayer reflects our common status as forgiven sinners who are dependent on God. Prayer demonstrates our concern for and commitment to one another. And yet prayer is often one of the first things that gets dropped from a youth group session or from the programme generally - usually because praying together is embarrassing or hard work. If our groups are Christian groups then we need to pray together and for one another. In fact, although it can be hard work getting a group praying, one of the best ways to grow in devotion to one another is by praying together.

  In the session outlines in this material we have included a 'Prayer Time' in each session. Sometimes this prayer time is directed and flows out of the Bible teaching; sometimes the prayer time is more general.

- **Praising God** – right at the heart of what it means to be Christian, both individually and corporately, is praising God. The psalmist overflows with praise to God, so do the early Christians in Acts 2, and so should the young people in our youth groups.

  Whenever young people meet together as Christians, they ought to be reminded of what God has done and encouraged to praise him. This may mean singing together, but for groups that would prefer not to sing, it will mean exploring other ways to express praise to God – perhaps in reading a Psalm together.

In the session outlines in this material we have included a 'Praise Time' in every session, and have made suggestions for both musical and non-musical youth groups.

- **Practical Care** – probably the most striking and challenging aspect of the early believers' life together, as described in Acts 2, is the practical care that they show for one another: "All the believers were together and had everything in common. Selling their possessions and goods, they gave to anyone as he had need."

  This practical and material care for each other ought to be reflected in all Christian youth groups, but rarely seems to be (in the western world at least). We need to give serious thought to how we care for one another practically and how that expresses itself in a youth group environment.

  In the session outlines in this material, we have not included suggestions for practical care because the way it works best will be different for each group, but practical care is an important part of what it means to be Christians together and we need to make sure that it is happening in our groups.

Seven Top Tips for Teaching the Bible to Young People

Tip 1 – Pray

It is God's word that we are teaching so we need his help to teach it. Ultimately he is the only one who can open our eyes to understand the Bible and open the eyes of the young people in our youth groups. So we need to pray when we are preparing, and while we are teaching and afterwards, that God would be at work through the Holy Spirit, helping people to listen, understand and put into practice what we are hearing from God's word.

Tip 2 – The Bible must set the agenda

If we are going to teach the Bible properly to young people we need to let the Bible do the teaching. We need to make sure that what we are teaching in a youth group session is what the passage teaches, and not what we, as the leaders, want to teach or what we think the young people need to hear.

Obviously, as we have planned the programme or picked the topics, we will have had some ideas about why we are teaching that particular topic, but when it actually comes down to dealing with the passage, we need to teach what it says and not what we want it to say. And we need to make sure that all of the elements that go to make up a youth group session work together in teaching the passage.

Tip 3 - Be clear without compromising

The key to good communication is clarity – see Nehemiah 8:8. And the key to clarity is knowing what you want to teach and working out how to teach it in a way that is appropriate, understandable and memorable.

Please Note: teaching clearly is not the same as being simplistic or dumbing-down; even the most difficult or complicated truths can be taught to young people if they are taught clearly. Inevitably this means that a good amount of work needs to be done in preparation to make sure that you, as the teacher, understand a passage or a topic. After all, if we do not understand a passage or a topic clearly, then what hope do we have of teaching it clearly to others?

Having done the hard work of understanding a passage or topic, we need then to think carefully about how we communicate that to our target audience. It is a useful exercise to ask whether we are teaching in a way that is appropriate, understandable and memorable.

Tip 4 – Good relationships help good teaching

It is generally true to say that good relationships facilitate good communication – see 1 Thessalonians 2:8. Of course, it is possible to communicate perfectly effectively with a complete stranger, but it is fair to say that, in normal circumstances, communication is easier where there is a good relationship in place. For instance, in trying to work out what level of communication is appropriate (see above) it helps to know the young people to whom we are trying to communicate, particularly in terms of language, illustration and application.

Some things to remember about developing relationships with young people:

• Make the Effort

Building relationships with young people takes time and effort, so we need to make sure that there is enough space in our programme for relationships to develop.

• Make Boundaries

Relationships flourish where there are clear and consistently enforced boundaries. It is possible to fall into the trap of thinking that being friends with a young person means allowing them to do what they like or never telling them off. Adult friendships do not work like that and neither do relationships between adults and young people. Young people need to know 'where they stand'; they need to feel secure in relationships and sometimes that means being firm in terms of discipline, boundaries, etc.

• Be Yourself

Young people want to relate to adults, so be yourself and do not try to be a teenager. Young people have plenty of friends of their own age, but what many are looking for, particularly in the transition between child and adult, is adults who will value and take an interest in them. Many teenagers, particularly if they are going through a period of conflict or non-communication with their parents, will look for supportive relationships with other adults. Interestingly, this relationship is often developed with a grandparent.

This means that youth and children's leaders do not have to pretend to be younger than they are. It also means that when we are putting together teams to work with children and young people, we do not have to limit ourselves to young leaders.

• Listen

Genuine relationships are two-way. So, in building relationships with young people, we need to listen and be appropriately honest and open. Paul talks about sharing his life with the Thessalonians (1 Thessalonians 2:8).

• Do not take yourself too seriously!

Because relationships are two-way, there is a possibility that we, as leaders, will be let down in a relationship. This is often the case with teenagers, who may not attach the same importance and significance to a relationship, so it is important that adult leaders do not take themselves too seriously.

Tip 5 - Be aware of the culture but not a slave to it

There is a school of thought that says that those who are involved in youth and children's work have to immerse themselves in the culture of young people – live how they live, dress how they dress, do what they do, etc. That is NOT what is being suggested here. Quite apart from anything else, youth culture is extremely difficult to define, partly because it is a mixture of all sorts of cultures and partly because no young person willingly fits into the 'typical' category.

There are, however, clearly differences between the world of young people and the world of adults. But, as we have seen already, young people want to relate to adults, and are therefore expecting that there will be a degree of cultural diversity. In fact, it is often this cultural diversity which adds value to the relationship – the fact that someone from a different world, culturally, is taking an interest in me and my world.

Having said all that, taking an interest in their lives and the world in which they live is an indication that we care for people, so it is worth being aware of the culture of the young people with whom we are working. So we might not like the music that they are into, but we can still ask about it. We may not watch the same programmes that they like, but we can still be aware of them.

In particular, if we are trying to communicate to teenagers, then it is worth learning about communication in the world of young people. Obviously, as we spend time with young people, we will begin to learn how they communicate.

However, there are a couple of ways that you can short-cut the process:

- Talk to school teachers. They are the ones who are specifically trained to communicate to young people. Good school teachers will have a wealth of knowledge and experience in communicating to teenagers.
- Watch television – particularly early in the evening, when programming and advertising is aimed specifically at young people. It is worth watching the advertisements every now and again, because advertisers know how to communicate to teenagers.

Tip 6 - Be varied in communication

One of the lessons from the culture of young people is the need to use variety in our communication. A very quick look at the advertisements or morning television shows us that young people are used to receiving a great deal of information, very quickly. And that information comes in a variety of forms – images, noises, words, instructions, actions, etc. Being varied in communication recognises, as we have seen already, that people learn or take in information differently.

Of course the Bible itself is full of variety in communication. Sometimes the communication is very visual – dreams, visions, parables or exciting narrative. Even as we read the passages, we are encouraged to visualise what is happening. Sometimes the communication is audible – the prophet speaks, the letter is read out, Jesus talks to somebody – and, again, even as we read these passages, it is as though we are listening in to what is being said. Sometimes the communication in the Bible is more physical – animal sacrifice, Jesus touching the leper, Thomas touching Jesus' hands and side, all communicating theological truth physically.

When teaching the Bible to young people it is important that we allow the richness and diversity of the Bible to be reflected in our teaching.

Tip 7 - Preparation is everything

Preparing a youth group session can be harder than preparing a talk or a study for adults. As well as doing all of the same preparation in terms of understanding the passage, you then have to work out how on earth you are going to communicate it to 14, 16, or 18 year olds.

The more time that leaders are able to take in preparing sessions, the better able they will be to teach young people effectively.

SERIES OVERVIEW
KEEP ON GOING

Lesson 1   Getting a Letter .... I Thessalonians 1:1–5:28
To listen to the letter as it was intended.

Lesson 2   A Genuine Conversion .... I Thessalonians 1:1-10
Thanking God that the Thessalonians are keeping going in a time of hardship.

Lesson 3   A Trustworthy Messenger .... I Thessalonians 2:1-16
Paul defends his message and method in Thessalonica.

Lesson 4   An Enduring Faith .... I Thessalonians 2:17–3:13
Paul cares for the Thessalonians and we should care for one another.

Lesson 5   A God-pleasing Life .... I Thessalonians 4:1-12
Living to please God.

Lesson 6   A Certain Hope .... I Thessalonians 4:13–5:11
Living in the knowledge that Jesus will come again to judge the world.

Lesson 7   Final Instructions .... I Thessalonians 5:12-28
How we should live as members of a Christian community.

Thessalonica was the capital city of the Roman province of Macedonia. It was a prosperous seaport, was on the main trade route from Istanbul and was an important communication and trading centre, being located at the junction of the Egnatian Way and the road leading north to the Danube. It was a bustling, pagan city, containing temples to the various Roman deities, as well as a Jewish synagogue, where Paul preached on his arrival (Acts 17:1-4).

The church was largely made up of Gentile converts and Paul's letter tells us that the problems they faced were persecution, temptation to sexual immorality, and concerns about the return of Jesus and the fate of those Christians who had already died. This makes it very relevant for our young people, who are constantly being pressurised to compromise in their Christian walk. If our group members are to keep on going as Christians they need to be convinced of the truth of the gospel, to understand how this affects the way they live, and to develop a network of prayer and contact to support each other through the week.

LESSON I

Getting a Letter

BIBLE READING

I Thessalonians 1:1–5:28

TEACHING POINT

To listen to the letter as it was intended.

LEADER'S PREPARATION

Thessalonica was a free city and the capital of the Roman province of Macedonia. It was a prosperous seaport and was on the main trade route from Istanbul. It was also an important communication and trading centre, being located at the junction of the Egnatian Way and the road leading north to the Danube. The city had a population of about 200,000, making it the largest city in Macedonia. Since Paul began his ministry in the Jewish synagogue (Acts 17:1-9) it is reasonable to assume that the new church included some Jews, but I Thessalonians 1:9-10 and Acts 17:4 indicate a large Gentile membership.

INFORMATION BOX

Background from Acts

1. Paul and Silas left Philippi and went to Thessalonica where they stayed for around 3 weeks, after which they were forced to leave by the Jews. Since Timothy is not mentioned, it is possible he stayed on in Philippi, joining Paul and Silas later in Berea (Acts 17:14).

2. Paul fled to Athens from Berea, leaving Silas and Timothy there.

3. Paul sent word back to Berea, instructing Silas and Timothy to join him as soon as possible.

4. Silas and Timothy must have rejoined Paul in Athens (see 1 Thessalonians 1:1; 3:1-2). Timothy was then sent back to Thessalonica to strengthen the new converts. Silas is not mentioned so it is possible he went back to Philippi when Timothy went to Thessalonica.

5. Paul went to Corinth where Silas and Timothy joined him. 1 Thessalonians was written from there, followed by 2 Thessalonians about 6 months later in (AD 51/52).

The first letter is generally dated as AD 51 and is one of Paul's earliest letters to the churches. (Some commentators suggest that Galatians may have been written earlier in approximately AD 48-49 shortly before the committee of enquiry met at Jerusalem to resolve the issue of the need for Christians to be circumcised (Acts 15:1-2).) It was written to encourage the early church in its trials and to reassure them about their future in Christ.

When Paul fled from Thessalonica after his brief stay, new converts from paganism were left in a time of persecution with little support. Paul wrote to encourage the Christians in their difficulties (1 Thessalonians 3:3-5), to give instructions about living as a Christian (4:1-8) and to reassure them of the certainty of Christ's second coming. The latter runs throughout the letter; every chapter ends with a reference to it and chapter 4 majors on the theme.

When the Thessalonian church received this letter it would have been read out to them. In order for the group to understand the impact of this get them to listen to a recording of the whole letter. It may need to be listened to more than once in order to pick up some of the themes running through the letter.

PLANNING THE SESSION

Welcome
Introduce yourselves
Start the meeting with prayer

Getting to Know You

Look for someone whose name starts with the same letter of the alphabet (or as near as possible) and ask them how they get a message to a friend.

Talk Time

Chat about how people keep in touch today. Take a poll to ascertain the favourite way of keeping in touch and of getting a message to someone.

Focus Time

The Letters Game. This is played like Consequences. Sit in a circle (or number of circles, depending on the size of the group). Give each person a piece of paper and a pen and ask them to complete a series of statements (see below). The statement is written at the top of the paper, then folded over to hide the writing and passed to the person on their left, ready for the next statement. They must avoid using rude words. At the end of the exercise the papers are unfolded and the resulting letters read out to the group.

Dear ....

I am writing because ....

I was surprised to hear ....

I am now feeling very ....

Please could you ....

Yours ....

Link into the Bible passage by pointing out that today they will be listening to a letter.

Bible Time

Start with an introduction to Thessalonica (see pages 18-20). If possible have two maps, one showing the area in the time of Paul and one showing it today.

If possible record the whole of 1 Thessalonians onto a CD prior to the session. Explain that the church at Thessalonica would have heard the letter read out in its entirety, and that is what you are going to do. Ask the group to listen carefully to try and work out why Paul was writing this letter. Play the recording.

If you are unable to get a recording of the letter ask a leader to read out the entire letter.

Ask the group to say why they think Paul wrote the letter, recording their answers on a flip chart. Keep the pages for use the following weeks.

Prayer Time

A leader closes in prayer, picking up on one or two things from the letter.

Praise Time

Musical groups – general songs (see www.kingswaysongs.com or www.emumusic.com for words and music).

Non-musical groups – read Psalm 100 as an antiphonal reading (two groups reading the verses turn and turn about). The first group reads verses 1 and 3, the second group verses 2 and 4, and both groups read verse 5.

Extra Ideas

Make a recording of the letter as a group.

Before listening to the letter ask the group to spot one or two big things that Paul raises in the letter for discussion afterwards.

LESSON 2

A Genuine Conversion

BIBLE READING

1 Thessalonians 1:1-10

TEACHING POINT

Thanking God that the Thessalonians are keeping going in the face of hardship.

LEADER'S PREPARATION

1:1   Paul, Silas and Timothy were the three gospel missionaries whom God used to found the church. Silas was a leader in the church at Jerusalem and was chosen by that church to go with Paul and Barnabas to Antioch to report the church's decision regarding what was required for Gentile converts to be accepted into fellowship (Acts 15:22-23). Following his disagreement with Barnabas over John Mark, Paul chose Silas to be his travelling companion (Acts 15:36-41). Silas was a Roman citizen and a prophet (Acts 15:32).

Timothy was a native of Lystra, in modern day Turkey, and was from a mixed background, with a Greek father and a mother who was a Jewish Christian (Acts 16:1). Paul invited him to go with him and Silas on his second missionary journey. Prior to their setting out Paul circumcised Timothy so that his Greek heritage would not be a hindrance (Acts 16:3). Silas and Timothy accompanied Paul through Macedonia and Achaia, so both were known to the Thessalonians.

QUESTIONS

What do we learn about Paul and the Thessalonian Christians?

1:1   The church was not a building, but a group of believers meeting in one another's homes. 'In God …' speaks of the church being under God's authority and in close relationship with him.

1:2   'Thank God for all of you' - this is a customary opening remark of Paul's, showing his love and concern for the church.

1:3   Paul prays for them continually.

Why does Paul thank God for them?

1:3   The Thessalonian Christians are demonstrating that they are keeping on going and growing.

What are the marks of a growing Christian?

1:3   They were working faithfully, labouring in love and enduring hopefully. For faith, love and hope cf. I Corinthians 13:13. For faith shown in action cf. James 2:14-17.

What four things did these new Christians do?

1:4   The reasons for Paul's conviction about the genuineness of the Thessalonians' faith are stated in verses 5-10.

1:5   'Our Gospel' - the only one that Paul preached, but it is God's Gospel (2:8) and also Christ's (3:2). Without the power of the Holy Spirit human words are useless.

1:6   They imitated Paul and Jesus - the example set first by Paul and then the church members was of the utmost importance in the spread of the Gospel. (As yet there was very little in the way of New Testament writings).

         Despite suffering, they welcomed the message with joy.

1:7   They became a model to other believers. (Greece was divided into the two provinces of Macedonia and Achaia.)

1:8   They spread the good news about Jesus. 'Everywhere' - a general term for all the places where Christians were to be found. Remember that this letter was only written a few months after the church was founded.

What might have stopped them believing in Jesus?

1:6   They were undergoing severe suffering. Paul, Silas and Timothy had encountered opposition from the Jews in Thessalonica and had been forced to depart after only 3 weeks, leaving behind a fledgling church (see Acts 17:5-9).

Instead, what was their attitude?

1:6   Joy, given by the Holy Spirit.

What are we told about Jesus?

1:10   Jesus is God's Son.

He is in heaven, from where he will return.

He was raised from the dead.

He rescues us from the coming wrath.

What was the only right way to live for him then?

1:9   To turn to him and serve him.

What should Christians be doing now?

1:10   Waiting for Jesus' return.

Welcome

- Introduce yourselves
- Start the meeting with prayer

Getting to Know You

Find someone wearing something the same colour and ask when have they kept going at something when they really wanted to give up?

Talk Time

Either have a general discussion about what helps you keep going as a Christian or chat about their school Christian Unions, how they help keep you going and how to keep them going.

Focus Time

Introduce the theme of perseverance. Get everyone to stand, holding their arms out to the side horizontal to the ground for as long as possible. If necessary, place heavy objects, such as books, on their hands. The winner is the last one left standing.

Another similar exercise is to lean against the wall in a sitting position with knees bent at right angles.

Bible Time

The Performance Poet

The Performance Poet introduces the theme of the study each week. Ideally the leader playing the part should be dressed in a beret, shades and goatee beard and should ridiculously overplay the role, taking the quality of their verse far too seriously.

> ### Even Though
> The apostle Paul gave thanks for his friends in Thessalonica
> Even though, as far as we know, none of them
> could play the harmonica.
> They accepted the gospel with joy and stayed keen
> Even though some of the people around them
> were quite mean.

See the worksheet on pages 56-59 for the Bible study questions and running order. Photocopy these pages for each group member for use during the Bible study. The worksheet contains questions for the group members to think about at home for next time.

Prayer Time

All together, read out 1 Thessalonians 1:2-3 as a prayer for each other.

Praise Time

Musical groups – use thank you songs, such as 'Give thanks to the Lord, our God and King' (see www.kingswaysongs.com or www.emumusic.com for words and music).

Non-musical groups – read Psalm 16 together.

Extra Ideas

Drawing it all together. On the back of a roll of wallpaper get members of the group to draw a picture representing what they have learned in the study. Cheap rolls of end-of-line wallpaper can be obtained from DIY stores. This will happen each week so that, by the end of the series, they will have built up a pictorial representation of the lessons from 1 Thessalonians.

If you have divided the group into smaller study groups, each small group can build up their own wallpaper collage and display them at the end of the session.

LESSON 3

A Trustworthy Messenger

BIBLE READING

1 Thessalonians 2:1-16

TEACHING POINT

Paul defends his message and method in Thessalonica.

LEADER'S PREPARATION

This passage is about Paul - how his message was validated by his life (v.1-12) and by its result (v.13-16). Many itinerant religious and philosophical teachers travelled around living off their hearers, so it was important for Paul to make clear that he was different from the others.

QUESTIONS

How difficult was it for Paul, Silas and Timothy to bring the gospel to the Thessalonians?

2:2   Very difficult. They had already suffered and been insulted in Philippi. (See Acts 16:19-40.)

What help did they have?

2:2   God's help gave them the courage they needed.

Why did they keep going?

2:4   Paul had been entrusted with the gospel by God.

Paul's motive for preaching was to please God, not men.

The Bible term 'hearts' means more than just emotions. It describes the control-centre of the personality, where we make our decisions and affirm our priorities So it includes the intellect and the will.

2:5-6   Paul's aim was never for personal profit nor was he seeking praise from men.

What did Paul and his friends do during their stay?

2:8   They shared their lives with them.

2:9   Paul worked hard, probably as a tentmaker (Acts 18:3), in his desire to show love and not to be a burden on the fledgling congregation. The Greeks despised manual work, viewing it as fit only for slaves, but Paul was not ashamed of doing it in order to further the cause of the gospel.

They preached the gospel of God to them.

How did Paul and his friends treat the Thessalonian Christians?

2:7,11   They cared for them as parents care for their children.

What was Paul's aim for these new Christians?

2:12   He wanted them to live lives worthy of God.

Which other people was Paul thinking of?

2:14   The Christians in Judea.

What had happened to them?

2:14-16   They had suffered from the hands of their countrymen, just as the Thessalonians were suffering from theirs (Acts 17:5-9). Paul encourages the Christians that suffering is a mark of the true church and not a sign that something has gone wrong.

What did the Thessalonians recognise Paul's message as?

2:13   The Thessalonians had recognised the gospel as being the word of God and having authority.

What does he say about the message to encourage them?

2:13   The message (the gospel) is at work in them.

PLANNING THE SESSION

Welcome
- Introduce yourselves
- Start the meeting with prayer

Getting to Know You
Divide into pairs using the following Pairs Game. Before the session make a list of famous pairs and write them on sticky address labels, one name per label. You need sufficient names for one per group member. Place a label on the forehead of each person and ask them to find their partners by asking each other questions, which can only be answered with 'yes' or 'no'. Once they have found their partners they need to find out who is the person they most admire and why.

Talk Time
Interview a leader or a group member about someone who has had a major influence on them.

Focus Time
Honey, I love you, but I just can't smile. This introduces the idea that Paul not only taught the message in Thessalonica, but also lived it out.

Stand in a circle with one person in the middle. The person in the middle goes up to someone (X), gets down on one knee and says, 'X, I love you, but I just can't smile.' X replies, 'Honey, you know I love you, but I just can't smile.' The point is not to smile. If X does so, they swap with the person in the middle and the game continues.

Link to the Bible study by pointing out that if your actions do not match your words you lose and end up in the middle. Will Paul's actions match up with his words?

Bible Time

The Performance Poet

For details see Lesson 2 (page 28).
Paul went to Thessalonica with a purpose
that might seem odd;
He came with the gospel entrusted to him by God.
He never gave in or altered his message;
Something you'll see as we study this passage.

See the worksheet on pages 60-63 for the Bible study questions and running order. Photocopy these pages for each group member for use during the Bible study. The worksheet contains questions for the group members to think about at home for next time. Remember to check who has done their homework.

Prayer Time

Either, get back into the pairs used for getting to know you and thank God for each other.

Or, in 3-4s share something that God has done for you or that you have learned from the passage and thank God for it.

Praise Time

Musical groups – use general thank you songs, such as 'Give thanks to the Lord, our God and King' (see www.kingswaysongs.com or www.emumusic.com for words and music).

Non-musical groups – read Psalm 27 together.

Extra Ideas

Drawing it all together. Continue with the pictorial representation of the lesson on a roll of wallpaper (see instructions in Lesson 2 (page 29).

LESSON 4

An Enduring Faith

BIBLE READING

1 Thessalonians 2:17 – 3:13

TEACHING POINT

Paul cares for the Thessalonians and we should care for one another.

LEADER'S PREPARATION

QUESTIONS

How hard did Paul try to get back to Thessalonica?

2:17   Paul had left Thessalonica earlier than he had planned.

Note the language used: 'made every effort', 'wanted to come . . . . . again and again' (v.18).

2:18   It may be that Paul had been forbidden to return, following the trouble he had with the city rulers (Acts 17:5-9).

2:19   The crown does not refer to a royal crown but to the wreath used on festive occasions or as the victor's garland in Greek games.

What does this tell us about Paul's care for the Thessalonians?

2:17   Note the language used: 'torn away', 'intense longing'

What does Paul pray?

3:11   He was praying and longing for the opportunity to visit them again. This prayer was answered during his third missionary journey (Acts 20:1-3).

Why was Paul so keen to get back to Thesalonica?

3:1   The 'we' is an editorial one, referring to Paul alone.

3:2-3   Paul was concerned about the Thessalonians' ability to keep going in the face of opposition, so sent Timothy to strengthen and encourage them.

3:3-4   Paul reassures the Thessalonians that their trials are not to be marvelled at, but expected.

What does this tell us about Paul's concern for the Thessalonians?

3:5   Belief in the power of God to preserve his people did not prevent Paul from feeling concern for the young Christians and did not stop him praying for them.

         Note the language: 'stand it no longer' (v.1,5).

When Paul could not get back to Thessalonica, what did he do?

3:2   He sent Timothy in his place.

3:9   Paul could have congratulated himself on work well done, but instead gives all the glory to God, thanking him for the Thessalonians.

3:10   Although the Thessalonians were standing firm and an example to other churches (1:7-8), they were not perfect in either Christian knowledge or behaviour. Paul prays constantly that he will be able to go to Thessalonica to supply what is lacking. In this letter Paul attempts to give them in writing what he had been unable to give them in person.

What did Timothy find out on his trip to Thessalonica?

3:6   Paul rejoices in the good news Timothy has brought back from Thessalonica. The good news is threefold – their faith, love and longing to see Paul.

3:8   Paul rejoices in the fact that the Thessalonians are standing firm in the Lord.

3:12-13   Paul prays that their love for each other will increase and that they will live godly lives. The reason given for this is being ready to meet Jesus when he returns.

PLANNING THE SESSION

Welcome
- Introduce yourselves
- Start the meeting with prayer

Getting to Know You
Find someone the same height (or as close as possible) and tell them about a friend you have not seen for sometime and are keen to see again.

Talk Time
Chat about visiting people in other countries. When have they done this? Ask 2-3 people to tell the group about the person they visited.

Focus Time
This game can be played indoors or outdoors as long as there is enough space and good places to hide. Mark out a base in the centre of the playing area. One person is 'It' and counts to 50 while everyone else hides. 'It' searches for the people hiding and when s/he finds someone they both race back to the base in the centre, the first one back shouting, '1-2-3-in!'

Link into the Bible study with being desperate to see someone.

Bible Time

The Performance Poet
For details see lesson 2 (page 28). (It might be worth explaining before you start that Thessalonica is a port on the Aegean Sea, which for the sake of this poem is part of the Mediterranean.)

Living to Please God

Paul was desperate to see all his friends in the Med.
He wanted to check that their faith was not dead.
In his efforts to see them he kept getting misled,
So he sent his friend Timothy instead.

See the worksheet on pages 64-67 for the Bible study questions and running order. Photocopy these pages for each group member for use during the Bible study. The worksheet contains questions for the group members to think about at home for next time. Remember to check who has done their homework.

Prayer Time

Get back into the pairs used for getting to know you and pray for each other.

Praise Time

Musical groups – use general thank you songs, such as 'Give thanks to the Lord, our God and King' (see www.kingswaysongs.com or www.emumusic.com for words and music).

Non-musical groups – read Psalm 34 together.

Extra Ideas

Drawing it all together. Continue with the pictorial representation of the lesson on a roll of wallpaper (see instructions in Lesson 2 (page 29).

LESSON 5

A God-pleasing Life

BIBLE READING

1 Thessalonians 4:1-12

TEACHING POINT

Living to please God.

LEADER'S PREPARATION

QUESTIONS

What was the problem faced by the Thessalonians?

4:3-6   The first problem Paul raises is freedom from sexual immorality. This needed emphasising because the highest pagan ethic fell far short of the Jewish and Christian standard. Sexual immorality refers to any form of sexual intercourse outside heterosexual marriage.

What instructions does Paul give them?

4:3   Be sanctified. Sanctification is the ongoing process of becoming more like Jesus.

Avoid sexual immorality.

4:4   Be self-controlled.

4:6   Do not wrong others or take advantage of them. By committing adultery the person is breaking up the marriage relationship and thus wronging his brother.

As Christians, what should be our aim?

4:1-2   The reason for living an ethical life is to please God. This instruction comes with God's authority, so it is not an option.

4:7   God calls us to live holy (set apart) lives.

What help is given us?

4:8   God gives his Holy Spirit to enable us to live holy lives. If we reject his instructions we are rejecting him.

Why should we bother to live this way?

4:3,7   This is what God wants.

4:6-7   These verses state God's view of sexual immorality. God will punish sinners.

What is Paul encouraged by?

4:9-10   Their love for one another. Love for fellow believers is another mark of the God-pleasing life.

What does Paul ask?

4:10   That they continue to love each other more and more.

What did Paul tell those Thessalonian Christians that thought they did not need to work?

4:11   Get to work. Work with your own hands refers to earning your own living. Some members of the church were so taken up with the second coming of Christ that they had stopped concerning themselves with earning their living and were sponging off fellow Christians. That this was an ongoing problem is seen in 2 Thessalonians 3:6-10.

These 3 commands deal with things that are potentially disruptive to the church fellowship. To lead a quiet life is not to be argumentative. Mind your own business means do not gossip.

What reasons does Paul give for living this way?

4:12   Outsiders will be attracted to Jesus.

Nobody will be burdened.

PLANNING THE SESSION

Welcome
- Introduce yourselves
- Start the meeting with prayer

Getting to Know You

Interview someone about the struggles they face in living to please God.

Talk Time

Ask for volunteers to tell the group what has been good about their week and others to tell about what has been bad.

Focus Time

Following Instructions. Photocopy page 45 for each person and ask them to follow the instructions through exactly.

Link into the Bible study with it being for their benefit to follow the instructions. Similarly, Paul's instructions on living to please God are for the Thessalonians' benefit.

Bible Time

The Performance Poet

For details see lesson 2 (page 28).

Living to Please God

Paul's implore,
Live lives pure
More and more,
Avoid 'Phwarr!'
Freedom, not Law.
Know the score.

See the worksheet on pages 68-71 for the Bible study questions and running order. Photocopy these pages for each group member for use during the Bible study. The worksheet contains questions for the group members to think about at home for next time.

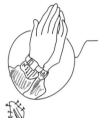

Prayer Time

In study groups, pray that each other will be enabled to live godly lives in the coming week.

Praise Time

Musical groups – use general thank you songs, such as 'Give thanks to the Lord, our God and King' (see www.kingswaysongs.com or www.emumusic.com for words and music).

Non-musical groups – read Psalm 103 together.

Extra Ideas

Drawing it all together. Continue with the pictorial representation of the lesson on a roll of wallpaper (see instructions in Lesson 2 (page 29).

FOLLOWING INSTRUCTIONS

Follow the instructions on this sheet for a reward.

1. Read all the instructions through before you begin.

2. Write your name in the top right hand corner of this instruction sheet.

3. Tear off a bit of the bottom left hand corner of this instruction sheet.

4. Do an impression of a cow.

5. Scrumple up the instruction sheet then open it out again.

6. Hop to one wall of the room and back again.

7. Repeat instruction 4.

8. Draw a circle around the word 'instruction' every time it appears on this sheet.

9. Clap 3 times as loudly as you can.

10. Do an impression of a dog.

11. Fold this sheet in half with the writing on the outside.

12. Read instruction 13 and say as loudly as you can, 'I am very, very silly.'

13. Ignore instructions 2-12, wait a few minutes and then trade this unblemished instruction sheet for a reward.

LESSON 6

A Certain Hope

BIBLE READING

1 Thessalonians 4:13 – 5:11

TEACHING POINT

Living in the knowledge that Jesus will come again to judge the world.

LEADER'S PREPARATION

Since Paul left Thessalonica two questions about the second coming had arisen:

1. Would those people who had already died lose out?
2. When was Jesus returning and was it worth planning for the future?

QUESTIONS

What is going to happen exactly?

4:16   Jesus will return from heaven.

There will be a loud command.

The dead Christians will rise.

4:17   All Christians will be gathered up into the air to be with Jesus forever.

'Meet' signifies the meeting with a great king or governor. When such a one approached a city the population and/or council would go out to meet him and escort him into the city.

What will make Jesus' return unmissable?

4:16   The loud command, the voice of the archangel and the trumpet call.

How can we be sure that these events will take place?

4:14   The death and resurrection of Jesus are the reason we can believe Paul's teaching on the second coming.

4:15   This is backed up by Jesus' own teaching - 'the Lord's own word' (see Matthew 24:30-31).

What will be the final result for Christians?

4:17   To be with God forever.

What two mistakes did Paul want his readers to avoid?

4:13   Being ignorant.

Grieving like unbelievers, those without hope.

What was his aim in writing like this?

4:18   To encourage them (see also 5:11).

What should Christians remember about the day Jesus returns?

5:1-3   Paul's teaching was always practical and never to satisfy idle curiosity. No one knows when Jesus will come again; it will be a surprise (cf. Matthew 24:3-14,36-44).

Whom will Jesus' return catch by surprise?

5:3   Those who think everything is fine.

How should Jesus' return affect the way we live now?

5:6-8   We should live as people of the light – alert and self-controlled. 'Others, who are asleep' refers to the unbelievers, not to the dead in Christ (4:14-15; 5:10).

Whom are the Thessalonians to go on trusting?

5:10   Jesus, who died for us.

Why does Paul say that Christians can look forward to Jesus' return?

5:9-10 Christians have received salvation.
        Christians will live forever with Jesus.

PLANNING THE SESSION

Welcome
- Introduce yourselves
- Start the meeting with prayer

Getting to Know You

Find someone with a birthday in the same month and ask them what is the thing they are most looking forward to at the moment.

Talk Time

Ask who has read something interesting in their Bible this week? If time permits, chat about what they are most looking forward to.

Focus Time

Hand out a piece of paper and pen to everyone and ask them to write down 3 headings – 1 year, 5 years, 40 years. Under each of the 3 headings ask them to write down, ON THEIR OWN, where they think they will be and what they think they will be doing in 1, 5 and 40 years' time.

Collect in all the pieces of paper, read out some of the future predictions and try to guess who wrote them.

Bible Time

> ### The Performance Poet
> For details see lesson 2 (page 28).
>
> Of the future the Thessalonians had fear,
> So Paul wrote to his friends who were dear.
> On Jesus' return he wanted them clear,
> So that they'd live as though it was near.

Use one of the wallpaper picture strips to recap on the letter so far.

See the worksheet on pages 72-75 for the Bible study questions and running order. Photocopy these pages for each group member for use during the Bible study. The worksheet contains questions for the group members to think about at home for next time. Remember to check who has done their homework.

Prayer Time

In study groups, pray that each other will be enabled to live godly lives in the coming week.

Praise Time

Musical groups – use general thank you songs, such as 'Give thanks to the Lord, our God and King' (see www.kingswaysongs.com or www.ecumusic.com for words and music).

Non-musical groups – read Psalm 98 together.

Extra Ideas

Drawing it all together. Continue with the pictorial representation of the lesson on a roll of wallpaper (see instructions in Lesson 2 (page 29).

LESSON 7

Final Instructions

BIBLE READING

1 Thessalonians 5:12-28

TEACHING POINT

How we should live as members of a Christian community.

LEADER'S PREPARATION

5:12   These verses are addressed to fellow Christians
        – 'brothers'.

QUESTIONS

**What commands does Paul give to the Thessalonian
Christians in v.12-15?**

These instructions are to do with the Christian's
relationships with those in the church.

5:12   Respect their hard-working leaders.

5:13   Live in peace with each other. 'Live in peace' - cf.
        4:11.

5:14 Warn those who are idle - cf. 4:11-12.

Encourage the timid.

Help the weak.

Be patient with everyone.

5:15 Make sure no-one pays back wrong for wrong, i.e. no retaliation.

Be kind to each other and to everyone else (this includes non-Christians).

What commands does Paul give them in v.16-22?

These verses deal with the Christian's relationship with God.

5:16 Be joyful always.

5:17 Pray continually.

5:18 Give thanks in all circumstances.

5:19 Don't put out the Spirit's fire. The Holy Spirit is active in Christians and the picture Paul gives is of a raging fire. It is wrong to try and suppress the Spirit's gifts, which are given for the good of the church (1 Corinthians 12:7).

5:20-21 The gift of prophecy. Prophets declared God's word to the people. The true prophet was recognised by his words coming true (1 Kings 17:22-24).

Paul calls on the Thessalonians to recognise the gift of prophecy and not disregard it. However, they were not to take prophecies at face value, but to test them to make sure they were from God. Anything that is not from God is bad and is to be jettisoned or avoided.

5:21-22   Hold on to the good and avoid every kind of evil.

What is encouraging about Paul's prayer?

5:23-24   Sanctification is an ongoing process and, although human effort is required, it comes about through God's faithfulness. These verses are not suggesting sinless perfection this side of heaven.

Welcome

- Introduce yourselves
- Start the meeting with prayer

Getting to Know You

Hand each group member a playing card. They have to find someone with the same face value and ask what is the best bit of advice they have ever been given.

Talk Time

Ask who has had a chance to chat to anyone about Jesus Christ or church this week. Discuss how to go about it.

Focus Time

Famous last words. From a book of famous last words, or a web-site, compile a list of famous last words and the people who said them. The aim is to try and match up the words with the person who said them. Do this in the pairs used for getting to know you.

Link into the study with looking at Paul's last words to the Thessalonians.

Bible Time

> ### The Performance Poet
> For details see Lesson 2 (page 28).
>
> Last words of Paul to Thessalonian mates;
> Instructions on living for God he relates.
> Getting on well with one another Paul rates.
> 'Walk closely with God,' he then states.

Use one of the wallpaper picture strips to recap on the letter so far.

See the worksheet on pages 76-79 for the Bible study questions and running order. Photocopy these pages for each group member for use during the Bible study. The worksheet contains questions for the group members to think about at home. Remember to check who has done their homework.

Prayer Time

In small groups, pray for a non-Christian friend and for the opportunity to talk to them about Jesus in the coming week.

Praise Time

Musical groups – use general thank you songs, such as 'Give thanks to the Lord, our God and King' (see www.kingswaysongs.com or www.emumusic.com for words and music).

Non-musical groups – read Psalm 67 together.

Extra Ideas

Drawing it all together. Continue with the pictorial representation of the lesson on a roll of wallpaper (see instructions in Lesson 2 (page 29).

Time to display the artistic achievements of the groups. Unravel the wallpaper and explain the drawings – hopefully this will provide a summary of what we have been learning from I Thessalonians.

A GENUINE CONVERSION

KEEP ON GOING WORKSHEET

Read 1 Thessalonians 1:1-3.

What do we learn about Paul and the Thessalonian Christians?

Why does Paul thank God for them? (v.3)
Draw out from this verse the marks of a growing Christian.

Think about on your own when you get a moment:
How much are you growing as a Christian?

Read 1 Thessalonians 1:4-8.

v.5 the gospel is about Jesus' death putting us right with God. See how the Thessalonians responded to the gospel . . .

What four things did these new Christians do? (v.6-8)

What might have stopped them believing in Jesus? (v.6)

Instead, what was their attitude? (v.6)

Think about on your own when you get a moment:
How would you have stood up in a similar situation?

How do you think 'the Lord's message' (the gospel) can
ring out from us?

A GENUINE CONVERSION

KEEP ON GOING WORKSHEET

Read 1 Thessalonians 1:9-10.

What are we told about Jesus?

What was the only right way to live for him then? (v.9)

What should Christians be doing now? (v.10)

Summary:

Paul is thanking God that the Thessalonian Christians were gladly trusting in Jesus, were keeping going despite opposition, were telling others and were ready for Jesus' return.

Could these things be said of us?

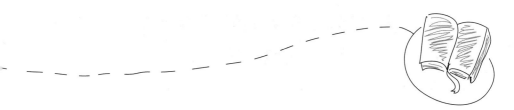

For Next Week:

Read 1 Thessalonians 1:1-10.

List all the things that Paul attributes to God in this passage.

In view of the fact that Paul is keen that the Thessalonians should stand firm, why does he remind them so much about what God has done?

How might remembering what God has done for us help us to keep on going?

A TRUSTWORTHY MESSENGER

KEEP ON GOING WORKSHEET

Read 1 Thessalonians 2:1-6.

Paul's point: 'Oi! we stuck at our job 'cos it was God we wanted to please.' See it in v.4?

How difficult was it for them? (v.2)

What help was there? (v.2)

Why did they keep going? (v.4-6)

Read 1 Thessalonians 2:7-12.

Paul's point: 'Oi! we did our best, sharing our lives and the gospel with you – we didn't just talk, but stayed and showed you how to live.'

What did Paul and his pals do during their stay? (v.8-9)

How did Paul and his pals treat the Thessalonian Christians? (v.7,11)

What was Paul's aim for these new Christians? (v.12)

Think about on your own when you get a moment:

Will you live a life worthy of God?

Read 1 Thessalonians 2:13-16.

Paul's point: 'Oi! I know it's been tough, but other people have been through it too.'

A TRUSTWORTHY MESSENGER

KEEP ON GOING WORKSHEET

Which other people was Paul thinking of? (v.14)

What had happened to them? (v.14-16)

But see how the Thessalonian Christians reacted to Paul's message . . .

What did they recognise it as? (v.13)

What does Paul say about the message to encourage them? (v.13)

Think about on your own when you get a moment:

Paul says, 'Don't give up!' What is there in today's passage to help you keep on going?

For next week:

Read Acts 17:1-10.

How would you describe Paul's visit to Thessalonica?

Paul visited Greece a second time (Acts 20), which is probably when he spent an extended period in Thessalonica. Why do you think Paul felt as strongly for the Thessalonians as he did?

What does this tell us about the way we should view other Christians?

AN ENDURING FAITH

KEEP ON GOING WORKSHEET

Read 1 Thessalonians 2:17-20.

Spot Quiz:

How hard did Paul try to get back to Thessalonica?

a. not a lot

b. it crossed his mind for when he had some spare holiday

c. he did try, but was too busy elsewhere

d. he was desperate

What does this tell us about Paul's care for the Thessalonians?

Look on to chapter 3 verse 11.

What does Paul pray?

Read 1 Thessalonians 3:1-5.

Spot Quiz:

Why was Paul so keen to get back to Thessalonica?

a.   he was lonely in Athens

b.   he was worried about them keeping going as Christians

c.   he liked landing himself in nightmare situations

d.   he could get good kebabs in Thessalonica

What does this tell us about Paul's care for the Thessalonians?

AN ENDURING FAITH

KEEP ON GOING WORKSHEET

Read 1 Thessalonians 3:6-13.

Spot Quiz:

When Paul couldn't get back to Thessalonica, what did he do?

a.   he sent Tim to find out how they were getting on spiritually

b.   he prayed constantly

c.   he kept thanking God for them

d.   he asked God to make it possible for him to go back

What did Tim find out on his trip to Thessalonica?

a.   they were standing firm in the faith

b.   they were unsettled because of opposition to their faith

c.   they didn't want to see Paul again

d.   they cared strongly for each other

What does all this have to say to us about the way that we look out for one another?

For next week:

Have a look again at Chapter 3 verses 3-7.

What is taught here about suffering for Jesus?

What did Paul have to endure?

Paul regularly reminded new Christians that it wasn't going to be easy.

What encourages Paul through his suffering?

Have you discovered that too?

A GOD-PLEASING LIFE

KEEP ON GOING WORKSHEET

When Timothy returned from Thessalonica, as well as reporting that they were standing firm as Christians, he also reported that there were a couple of problems they needed help with.

PROBLEM I

Read 1 Thessalonians 4:1-8

What was the problem facing the Thessalonians?

Jot down the instructions Paul gives them.

As Christians, what should be our aim? (v.1,7)

What help is given us? (v.8)

Why should we bother to live this way? (v.3,6-7)

Self-control? Not easy, but we're not on our own; God lives by his Spirit in those who trust him . . . and he'll help us to live to please him. Think about when you get a moment:

How good is your self-control?

What areas could see some improvement – whether in thoughts, words or behaviour?

Are there situations we should avoid to help us remain self-controlled?

A GOD-PLEASING LIFE

KEEP ON GOING WORKSHEET

PROBLEM 2

Read 1 Thessalonians 4:9-12.

Spot Quiz:

What is Paul encouraged by? (v.9-10a)

What does Paul ask? (v.10b)

What did he tell those Thessalonian Christians who thought they didn't need to do any work? (v.11)

What are the two reasons for living that way? (v.12)

Think about when you get a moment:

Does the way you work help point people to Jesus?

How are you going to make progress in pleasing God?

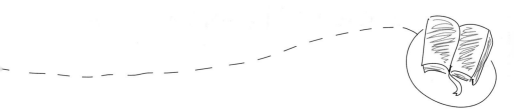

For next week:

Read again 4:1-2, 9-10.

See the phrase that gets repeated . . .

What's Paul keen for the Thessalonian Christians to do?

i.e. there's always further progress to make . . .

v.11 is literally, 'make it your ambition to have no ambition',

i.e. calm down and get on with some work humbly and quietly.

How does this alter your thinking about jobs, career, etc?

Does your daily life win the respect of outsiders?

A CERTAIN HOPE

KEEP ON GOING WORKSHEET

JUST TO SET THE SCENE . . .

Paul is explaining to the Thessalonians about the greatest event of all time – Jesus' second coming, when Jesus will return and Christians will be with him forever.

The Christians in Thessalonica are worried about what has happened to their friends who have died. Paul gives them, and us, a clear view of what the future holds.

Read 1 Thessalonians 4:13-18.

What's going to happen exactly? (v.16-17)

What will make Jesus' return unmissable? (v.16)

How can we be sure that these events will take place? (v.14)

What will be the final result for Christians? (v.17b)

What two mistakes did Paul want his readers to avoid? (v.13)

What was his aim in writing like this? (v.18)

Think about when you get a moment: How does this future prospect strike you?

How should this future certainty affect the way we live now?

A CERTAIN HOPE

KEEP ON GOING WORKSHEET

Read 1 Thessalonians 5:1-3.

Paul tells them not to worry about exactly when Jesus will return.

Instead, what should Christians remember about the day Jesus returns? (v.2-3)

Whom will Jesus' return catch by surprise? (v.3)

Read 1 Thessalonians 5:4-8.

How should Jesus' return affect the way we live now? (v.6-8)

Read 1 Thessalonians 5:9-11.

Whom are the Thessalonians to go on trusting? (v.10)

Why does Paul say that Christians can look forward to Jesus' return? (v.9-10)

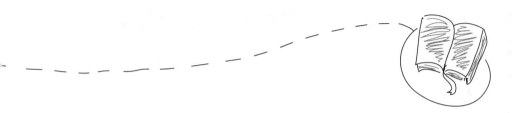

For next week:

Read 1 Thessalonians 4:13.

What makes Christians different from other people when it comes to facing up to the death of Christian friends and family?

Read 1 Thessalonians 5:4-11.

Are you, honestly, ready for Jesus' return?

Is your behaviour like that called for in v.8?

Put into your own words what Jesus has done for us in v.9-10.

FINAL INSTRUCTIONS

KEEP ON GOING WORKSHEET

Final Instructions (1 Thessalonians 5:12-28)

Last week Paul encouraged the Thessalonian Christians to be ready for Jesus' return. This week he is giving them a final checklist to make sure that they are ready . . .

First, they need to sort out their relationships with other people.

Read 1 Thessalonians 5:12-15.

List all the commands that Paul gives to the Thessalonian Christians.

What is one way that we could show more respect for our Christian leaders?

Can we think of a Christian friend we could encourage?

Can we think of one person that we could be more patient with?

Think about when you get a moment:

How do your relationships reflect your 'readiness' for Jesus' return?

Read 1 Thessalonians 5:16-28.

Again, list all the commands that Paul gives to the Thessalonian Christians.

Which do you find the hardest?

FiNAL iNSTRUCTiONS

KEEP ON GOING WORKSHEET

Look at the 3 commands in v.16-19.

How often do you behave like this?

How are you getting on then?

What is encouraging about Paul's prayer? (v.23-24)

At home:

Read 1 Thessalonians 5:12-28 again.

Bowled over by the number of commands? Well, take heart from Paul's prayer (v.23) and God's promise (v.24).

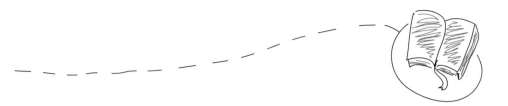

How do these encourage you to get started in obeying what's here?

Is there any one command that stands out?

Look back over 1 Thessalonians and think:

What have I learned about Jesus?

What must I copy from Paul and the Thessalonians?

What have I learned that I need to change?

CHRISTIAN FOCUS PUBLICATIONS

Christian Focus | Christian Heritage | CF4K | Mentor

Christian Focus Publications publishes books for adults and children under its four main imprints: Christian Focus, Christian Heritage, CF4K and Mentor. Our books reflect that God's word is reliable and Jesus is the way to know him, and live for ever with him.

Our children's publication list includes a Sunday school curriculum that covers pre-school to early teens; puzzle and activity books. We also publish personal and family devotional titles, biographies and inspirational stories that children will love.

If you are looking for quality Bible teaching for children then we have an excellent range of Bible story and age specific theological books.

From pre-school to teenage fiction, we have it covered!

Find us at our web page:
www.christianfocus.com

CF4•K
Because you're never
too young to know Jesus